X-Treme Sports

Windsurfing

Stephanie F. Hedlund

ABDO Publishing Company

visit us at
www.abdopub.com

Published by ABDO Publishing Company, 4940 Viking Drive, Edina, Minnesota 55435.
Copyright © 2003 by Abdo Consulting Group, Inc. International copyrights reserved in all
countries. No part of this book may be reproduced in any form without written permission from
the publisher.

Printed in the United States.

Cover Photo: Corbis
Interior Photos: Corbis pp. 4, 5, 7, 8-9, 10, 11, 12, 14-15, 17, 19, 21, 25, 26-27, 28, 29, 31

Editors: Kate A. Conley, Jennifer R. Krueger
Art Direction: Neil Klinepier

Library of Congress Cataloging-in-Publication Data

Hedlund, Stephanie F., 1977-
  Windsurfing / Stephanie F. Hedlund.
    p. cm. -- (X-treme sports)
  Includes index.
  Summary: Examines the history, techniques, racing events, and more of windsurfing.
  ISBN 1-57765-931-7 656
  1. Windsurfing--Juvenile literature. [1. Windsurfing.] I. Title. II. Title: Wind surfing.
III. Series.

  GV811.63. W56 H835 2003
  797.3'3--dc21
                                                    2002026091

Contents

Windsurfing

Windsurfing, also called sailboarding, is a combination of sailing and surfing. In this sport, a sail is attached to a surfboard. This allows people of any age or physical ability to sail on their own. Windsurfing is a fairly new sport. But in a short time, it has become very popular.

There are two types of windsurfing, light-wind and high-wind. Athletes with little experience can perform the light-wind type. However, high-wind windsurfing is for advanced athletes. Both types offer competitions with different difficulty levels.

The best way to learn windsurfing basics is by attending a school. In a few days, even the least athletic person can learn to windsurf. Books, magazine articles, and instructors are great for helping to learn difficult moves.

Windsurfing is challenging. This sport takes practice and patience whether you are cruising, slalom racing, or wavesailing. No matter what kind of windsurfing you choose, it can be a fun activity for the whole family!

Windsurfing History

Some people believe windsurfing began in the ancient civilizations of South America. There, people may have used rafts with masts to travel along the Amazon River. However, the first well-known sailboard appeared in the 1960s.

In 1964, Newman Darby invented what he called a sailboard. He is the first prominent inventor of windsurfing. He attached a sail to a rectangular board. On his sailboard, Darby could use the wind to travel on the water. He could also steer without a **rudder**.

Darby, his wife, and his brother began Darby Industries. The company began producing sailboards. But they never applied for a patent. In 1965, they made the first universal joint that attached a sail to a board. The universal joint allowed the sail to move in any direction. With this invention, sailboarding became much easier.

Darby and his company began promoting the sailboard. *Popular Science* published a four-page article about it in 1965. Soon, Darby Industries began receiving letters from around the world.

Windsurfing didn't catch on, however. Darby Industries stopped making sailboards in the late 1960s. They had to stop because not enough people wanted to buy sailboards. But that would soon change.

In 1968, Jim Drake and Hoyle Schweitzer received the first patent for a sailboard. Drake, a sailor, and Schweitzer, a surfer, had combined their sports into one. They called it windsurfing and began producing the Windsurfer.

The Windsurfer was the first **mass-produced** sailboard. It had a wide board, a universal joint, and a sail. The Windsurfer was based on Darby's design. For this reason, Drake and Schweitzer credited Darby with inventing it.

Schweitzer and his wife began promoting the Windsurfer. They went to many boat shows in North America to expose the sport. They even set up a board that allowed people to try windsurfing on dry land! This brought windsurfing to an even broader group of people.

Newman Darby first got the idea for his sailboard after watching his wife test a boat he had built. The boat had no rudder, so she steered the boat by moving the sail with her hands. Then, Darby and his wife decided to attach the sail to a surfboard, creating the modern sailboard.

Windsurfing caught on quickly outside of the United States. In the early 1970s, windsurfing was introduced in Europe. Schweitzer also allowed manufacturers in Japan, Australia, and Africa to produce the Windsurfer.

European manufacturers began altering the Windsurfer. They improved the boards and sails by using new materials. Soon, one in three European households had a sailboard. From 1979 to 1984, Europeans bought more than 1 million sailboards.

In the early 1980s, windsurfing began to grow in the United States, too. Americans began buying the European sailboards. They also developed versions of their own. Americans used footstraps, shorter boards, and different types of sails. These items made it easier to race and perform jumps and tricks.

Windsurfing competitions also became popular. [...]
windsurfers participated in the first world champion[...]
windsurfing. Windsurfing became an official event fo[...]
the 1984 Olympic Games in Los Angeles, California. In 1992, a women's event was added to the Olympic Games.

Today, the Professional Windsurfers Association (PWA) World Tour involves competitors from all over the

U.S. windsurfer Mike Gebhardt races on Sydney Harbor in 2000.

world. Many countries have windsurfing associations to regulate competitions. Windsurfing has become one of the world's fastest-growing sports. More than 15 million people worldwide enjoy windsurfing.

Equipment

There are two pieces of equipment needed to begin windsurfing. They are a board and a rig. A board is made of either plastic or **fiberglass**. A rig includes a sail, a mast, and a boom. **Accessories** are also important purchases for any windsurfer.

Boards

There are two basic types of boards. They are long boards and short boards.

Long boards include any board that is between 10 feet (3 m) and 12 feet, 6 inches (4 m) long. They are best for light-wind windsurfing and for beginners because they have a centerboard. A centerboard stabilizes the board. Long boards are also used for racing and are sometimes called courseboards.

Short boards are less than 10 feet (3 m) long. They do not have a centerboard, so they are less stable. Short boards are used for high-wind windsurfing and for doing tricks. Beginners should not use these boards because they are difficult to sail.

Each board has a fin under its tail. The fin helps keep the board sailing straight. Each board also has a mast track. This allows the mast to slide along the length of the board.

Opposite page: This board's fin helps direct it in the water. The windsurfer holds the boom to direct the sail.

Rigs

The sail, mast, and boom connect to form the rig. Manufacturers sell each part of the rig separately. But windsurfers can also buy a complete package. The package often includes both the board and the rig.

There are four basic types of sails. They are beginner, recreational, racing, and wave sails. Each sail has a different use and **unique** features.

Beginner sails are good for light-wind windsurfing. They are light and easy to lift out of the water. Recreational sails are used in both types of windsurfing. These sails are easier to move in the wind. Racing sails are for windsurfing at high speeds. They are rounded and closer to the board. This helps them gain power and speed. The wave sail is used in the open sea. It is the smallest type of sail. It is powerful, but easy to control.

The mast is a lightweight rod that attaches the sail to the board. The standard mast is 181 inches (460 cm) long. It fits onto the mast base. The mast base includes a universal joint. It fits into the mast track on the board.

The boom is a tube that is used to direct the sail. The boom clamps to the mast at shoulder height. It also attaches to the sail with a rope. The boom allows the windsurfer to swing the sail and **maneuver** the board.

Accessories

In addition to a board and a rig, windsurfers also use **accessories**. Anyone who participates in water sports must wear a life jacket. These flotation devices are important for safety in deep water.

Footstraps, harnesses, **wet suits**, booties, and gloves can also be purchased for windsurfing. Footstraps fasten the windsurfer's feet to the board. This allows a person to jump and do other tricks. However, beginners will not find footstraps useful until they improve their skills.

Harnesses let windsurfers use their bodies to hold up the sail. This allows their arms to rest, which means they can stay on the water longer. Harnesses are often used for racing and wavesailing.

Wet suits, gloves, and booties are also important for windsurfers. Wet suits protect the body from many dangers, including cold water, sunburn, and cuts. Gloves and booties also protect a windsurfer's hands and feet from cuts. This water gear works best if it fits properly.

This windsurfer wears a wet suit, life jacket, and gloves for protection.

Rules

Basic rules for windsurfing are easy to follow. Collisions and injuries can be avoided if you follow these simple rules.

First, never leave your board. It is a stable flotation device, and it can get you back to shore. If you are unable to sail to shore, disconnect your mast. Next, wrap your sail around it, and place it on your board. You can then paddle back to shore.

Second, know and prepare for the site conditions. Check weather reports, know beach traffic patterns, and wear appropriate clothing.

Third, know how to use the **international distress signal**. Sit on the board. Wave your arms above your head and then down to your sides. This shows you need help.

Finally, know and use the correct **right-of-way** rules for windsurfing. Following these rules helps avoid crashes and injuries.

Lingo

freestyle

This style involves doing tricks on a board, sometimes in competition.

centerboard

The centerboard is a large fin on the bottom of the board. It keeps the board stable.

jibe

To jibe is to turn the tail of the board into the wind.

Beaufort Scale

This scale is a method of measuring wind strength. The scale rates the wind from 0 to 12.

barrel roll

A barrel roll is a backward loop done into the wind.

rails

The edges of the board are called the rails.

carve

To carve is to turn quickly by pressing the inside rail.

aerial

An aerial is any trick performed in midair.

22

cruising

Cruising is sailing from point to point. It is the simplest form of windsurfing.

light-wind windsurfing

This type of sailing is done in wind speeds of 10 knots or fewer. Cruising is done in light-wind conditions.

high-wind windsurfing

This type of sailing is done in wind speeds of 15 to 25 knots. It is performed by advanced windsurfers.

plane

To plane is to sail on top of the water, instead of plowing through it.

knot

A knot is one nautical mile per hour. Nautical miles are used to measure sea and air distances.

cut back

In wavesailing, a cut back is a sudden move toward the bottom of a wave.

bump-and-jump

Bump-and-jump windsurfing refers to high-wind sailing that involves jumps and turns at high speeds.

slalom

To slalom is to do high-wind windsurfing at high speeds. Usually slalom sailing involves racing a course.

sheeting

Sheeting is changing the angle of the sail by pushing or pulling with the back hand.

universal joint

This type of joint allows a windsurfer to move the sail in any direction.

uphaul

The uphaul is the rope used to raise the rig from the water.

tail

The tail is the back of the board. It is also called the stern.

wavesailing

Wavesailing is riding breaking waves parallel to the beach at high speeds. It is the most difficult form of windsurfing.

waterstart

A waterstart is starting from the water by letting the sail pull the windsurfer onto the board.

tacking

Tacking is turning by facing into the wind and stepping around the sail.

Many of the terms used in windsurfing are also used in surfing and sailing. For example, surfers also perform aerial tricks and cut backs. Sailors also use the term jibe to describe turning the boat downwind.

Windsurfing Today

Today, windsurfing is a popular, competitive sport. The PWA World Tour is held each year. Windsurfers from around the world compete in course races, slalom races, and freestyle competitions. Windsurfing is also an Olympic sport.

With this popularity, the sport has many important leaders. In 2001, Roger Jackson won the Windsurfer of the Year Award. He has introduced hundreds of young people to the sport. He has also helped disabled children learn to sail and windsurf.

Robby Naish is also an important figure in windsurfing. He won his first world championship when he was 13 years old. He was the youngest person ever to win.

Naish continued touring. He has won five overall PWA **titles**. He also won three World Championship Wave titles. Many people consider Naish the greatest windsurfer in the sport's history.

Other important windsurfers include Nik Baker, Matt Pritchard, Daida Moreno, and Iballa Moreno. Baker and Pritchard compete in the men's freestyle and other events. Daida and Iballa Moreno are sisters who dominate the women's competitions.

Windsurfing is an enjoyable sport for anyone, regardless of age or physical ability. It can be a challenging **workout**. But windsurfing is gaining popularity around the world. That's because it's an exciting sport that captures the fun of the wind and water.

Glossary

accessory - a small part added to improve something larger.

fiberglass - a material made of threads of glass.

international distress signal - a widely understood way to request help when in danger.

maneuver - to move or manage.

mass-produce - to produce large numbers of an item, usually using machines.

right-of-way - the right to go first.

rudder - a piece attached to the back of a boat that can be turned to change the boat's direction. Sailboards do not have rudders.

title - relating to or involving a championship competition or prize.

unique - being the only one of its kind.

wet suit - a tight, waterproof suit that keeps the body warm.

workout - a period of exercise and practice.

Web Sites

Would you like to learn more about windsurfing? Please visit **www.abdopub.com** to find up-to-date Web site links about this sport and its competitions. These links are routinely monitored and updated to provide the most current information available.

Index